Vincent van Gogh by Ernest Raboff and Adeline Peter

Art for Children

Cover: The Postman
Kröller-Müller Foundation, Otterlo

With his strong face, great curling beard and firm, upright stance, Monsieur Roulin looks proud and confident—more like a general than a postman!

The authority in his face, with its thoughtful eyes, and the sturdiness of his shoulders contrast with the gay, brilliantly patterned background. The flowers reflect the countryside where he lived. Perhaps they express something too of his open-hearted nature, for he was a kind man and always a good friend to van Gogh.

The Road to Tarascon   Kunsthaus, Zürich

Portrait of Camille Roulin   Collection of Mr and Mrs Rodolphe Meyer de Schauensee, Devon, Pennsylvania

THE AUTHOR

Ernest Raboff, artist, art critic, and art dealer, has been associated with art and artists for forty years.

As a young poet, he studied art in France and Italy, where he came in contact with Picasso, Léger, and the sculptor Giacometti. From Paris, Raboff travelled to Sweden where he lectured on the art of the United States. His illustrated book of poetry received a special award as Book of the Year in Sweden.

Mr Raboff has travelled to and studied in most of the great museums of the world, including the Tate and the National Gallery, the Uffizi, the Prado, the Louvre, the Jerusalem International, the Rijksmuseum, and the National Museum of Stockholm. Over the years working as a writer interested in art, a collector and an art dealer, he has become well-known to the international art community. His greatest pleasure is to guide children through the magic world of art and artists.

Ms. Adeline Peter, Mr Raboff's collaborator, received her art education in Pennsylvania and California.

Dedicated to Mildred and Joe Raboff and their children, my
cousins, Paul Raboff and Flora Golden

© 1980 by Gemini Smith Inc. and Ernest Raboff

First published in Great Britain 1980 by Ernest Benn Limited
25 New Street Square, London EC4A 3JA and Sovereign Way, Tonbridge, Kent TN9 1RW

Printed in Japan by Toppan

ISBN 0 510 00103 3

Vincent van Gogh by Ernest Raboff
and Adeline Peter

Art for Children

A GEMINI-SMITH BOOK
EDITED BY BRADLEY SMITH

Ernest Benn
LONDON & TONBRIDGE

VINCENT VAN GOGH was born in Groot-Zundert, Holland on 30th March, 1853. His father was a minister of the Dutch Reformed Church and his mother came from a family of bookbinders. Vincent, their eldest child, had a brother, Theo, and three sisters.

As a young boy he showed no particular interest in drawing or painting but preferred running free in the countryside, chasing after butterflies and beetles and hunting for birds' nests. Often he was a lonely child and a difficult one too, partly because of his nature and partly because, though he knew his parents loved him, he felt they did not understand him. Only Theo, his young brother whom he loved dearly, was his trusted friend in the family. It was with Theo more than with anyone else, that Vincent all his life shared his griefs, joys and ideas on every subject.

In 1864, at the age of 11, Vincent was sent away to boarding school. He had become rather too troublesome for his parents to keep at home. In 1869, through the help of one of his uncles, Vincent began work as an assistant at the Goupil Gallery in The Hague. There he came into contact with and admired the work of the famous French painter Jean François Millet. In 1873 he transferred to the London branch of Goupil's and then later moved to their main branch in Paris. For several years he travelled back and forth, living variously in England, Paris, Etten, The Hague, Drenthe, Nuenen and Antwerp.

Cornfield and Cypress Trees, 1889   National Gallery, London

Strong religious feelings led him in 1877 to decide to follow his father and become a clergyman. His studies were unsuccessful though and a year later he left for the Borinage, a coal mining district of Belgium, hoping, at least, to be a lay preacher. This venture was not a success either but there, in 1879, he made the very important discovery that he must become a painter. However it was much later, in 1886, that he arrived in Paris and discovered the brilliant colours and daring freedom of expression of the Impressionists.

In Paris, too, van Gogh met Paul Gauguin and was greatly impressed by him, both as a man and a painter. It was due to Gauguin's influence that in 1888 he decided to go to Arles in the south of France. It was there that the purity of light and brilliance of colours of the region released the full force of his creative genius.

From 1888 till his death in 1890, van Gogh worked furiously, driving himself without rest. He applied paint to canvas with reckless energy which is evident, still, in every brushstroke. Often, he went without food in order to pay for paints and canvas with what little money he had.

Vincent van Gogh's life for the most part was far from happy. His work received little or no recognition during his lifetime, apart from a few fellow painters and his brother, Theo. His difficult temperament made easy loving relationships with others almost impossible. He was only 37 when he committed suicide. Only through his paintings and the remarkable letters he wrote to his brother, Theo, could he express his real feelings and ideas.

Self-portrait   Stedelijk Museum, Amsterdam

THE HARVEST

During 1888 whilst staying in Arles in the south of France, van Gogh painted a series of landscapes depicting the seasons. This one tells a story about late summertime. The whole canvas glows with rich oranges, yellows, blues and greens. The grain is ripe and harvest has just begun. The hay has been mown and we can see a figure standing on a cart pitching forkfuls into a tall barn loft.

There is a wonderful feeling of light, space and distance. Warm sunshine from a cloudless sky catches the roofs and sides of buildings and the standing golden corn. The air is so clean and clear our eye wanders effortlessly through the fields, past the houses and barns to the distant and mysterious mountains on the horizon.

The landscape seems so vast that at first we hardly notice the tiny figures going about their daily business. Like the buildings, the people have been positioned in the composition further and further away from one another and from our eye. They are like stepping stones and take us deeper and deeper into the picture.

Right at the centre of the composition van Gogh places an exaggeratedly large blue cart. The spokes of the wheel radiate outwards to all parts of the landscape and at the same time draw them in towards the hub which is the focal point of the picture.

Landscape with Windmill   Gemeente Museum, Amsterdam

The Harvest   Stedelijk Museum, Amsterdam

DAISIES AND ANEMONES

This simple vase of flowers vibrates with colour and life.

A picture of objects seen from a short distance is called a 'still life' but there is nothing static about this composition. The flowers seem to be bursting out of their vase and even the background made of dots and dashes of thick paint pulsates with energy. Notice how directly the paint is applied to the canvas so that, for instance, a single brushstroke clearly defines a whole petal.

Van Gogh painted this picture in Paris where he had recently seen, for the first time, the work of the Impressionists. He was very excited by their use of brilliant colour harmonies and their passion for light.

Garden Entrance   Gemeente Museum, Amsterdam

Daisies and Anemones, 1887   Kröller-Müller Foundation, Otterlo

VINCENT'S BEDROOM AT ARLES

This painting makes us feel we are actually right inside van Gogh's bedroom and not just looking into it from the outside.

This bedroom was in his 'little yellow house' in Arles which he had so excitedly painted and decorated inside and out. The materials he needed took all his money and for four days he lived on nothing but coffee and dry bread. He often went without food in this way, preferring always to spend the little cash he had on paints and canvas.

The two self-portraits on the wall were given to him by his painter friends, Emile Bernard and Paul Gauguin. Van Gogh greatly admired Gauguin, who later came to stay in another room in the 'little yellow house' which van Gogh had specially prepared for him.

The room is quiet, the colours warm and restful. Without hurrying, we can look carefully at each possession in turn. Soon it is easy to imagine either lying on the bed, sitting on one of the chairs or standing to open the windows.

All the objects in the room, apart from the clothes on pegs, are placed apart from one another and do not overlap. The bed, the chairs, the table, the mirror and even the towel hanging from a nail are all equally important. We feel that van Gogh knows and loves them all and that they belong only to him and to no one else.

Vincent's House at Arles   Vincent van Gogh Museum, Amsterdam

Vincent's Bedroom at Arles   The Louvre, Paris

GAUGUIN'S ARMCHAIR

Dish, Knives and Kettle
Van Gogh Museum, Amsterdam

Van Gogh was a lonely man throughout his life and any friendship was a rare and precious thing to him. When Gauguin agreed to come to stay and work with him in his 'little yellow house' he was very happy and excited. He dreamed of founding with his friend a centre for Impressionist painters in his home in Arles.

When Gauguin did arrive to stay with van Gogh in Arles, all went well for a while. Before long though, their relationship began to be quarrelsome. Van Gogh's behaviour became increasingly strange and when finally he threatened his friend with an open razor, Gauguin decided it was time to leave. It was immediately after this occasion, when still in a deranged state of mind, that van Gogh, with this same razor, cut off part of his left ear.

This picture is only of a chair but it tells us a great deal about the man who sat in it and of van Gogh's feelings about him. Gauguin was a large powerful man who dominated his surroundings, so his chair is solid, robust and fills the canvas. Gauguin had 'style' and an easy going nature so the chair's arms, legs and backrest are flamboyantly curved and generous in proportion. Gauguin had the natural calm and authority of a big man so the legs of the chair are strong, widely spread and stable.

The green of the wall echoed in the colour of the chair's seat, the brown of the chair itself, blending with the warmer tones of the carpet, and the gently hissing gas lamp all combine to convey friendliness and a sense of security. The burning candle and the books tell us that Gauguin is nearby and will soon return.

Portrait of the Artist with a Bandaged Ear, 1889
Courtauld Institute Galleries, London

Gauguin's Armchair   Stedelijk Museum, Amsterdam

Study of 8 Hands   Van Gogh Museum, Amsterdam

THE ZOUAVE

(Pronounced zoo-ah-vay). This portrait is of a French soldier from North Africa. These soldiers were quartered in barracks nearby.

The figure is full of confidence, relaxed yet in readiness for immediate action if necessary. The eyes are watchful and look directly out at us.

The bold dark head wearing a jaunty tasselled cap, the decorated jacket and blue cummerbund stand out strongly against a plain white background. The knees under the red costume jut out arrogantly almost at right angles. The feet are planted very squarely on the tiled floor and seem enormous in comparison with his hands and head. The lower part of his body, the exaggeratedly long thighs and the over large feet give the personality of the soldier a thrusting aggressive quality. This feeling is emphasised by the angled direction of the tiles and the strong positive vertical made by the doorway or curtain to the right.

Van Gogh was interested above all in achieving an expression of the whole personality in a portrait rather than a photographic likeness.

The Zouave   Guggenheim Museum, New York

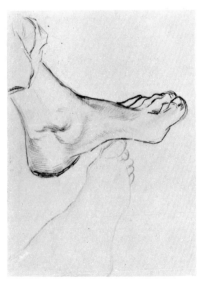

Study of Feet,   Van Gogh Museum, Amsterdam

The Zouave

PEAR TREE IN BLOSSOM

The Owl
Van Gogh Museum, Amsterdam

Van Gogh, together with many fellow artists at the time, greatly admired Japanese prints made from woodcuts. *Pear Tree in Blossom* with its combination of simplicity, strength and, at the same time, delicacy, clearly shows their influence.

The young tree is bursting with vitality. On the fragile, twisting branches the blossoms seem to explode with life. The slender stem, even though firmly rooted in the ground, hardly looks able to support such abundance. Notice the orange butterfly about to alight on one of the blossoms.

Spring lasts only a short while and van Gogh captures a sense of special urgency, the feeling that there is no time to lose. Every brushstroke on the canvas has been applied swiftly and without hesitation.

Van Gogh's painting makes us aware of the immense force in all growing things, their energy caught from the sun above and their nourishment drawn from the earth beneath.

The blue of the sky and the warm pink and orange colours glowing in the bright sunshine are full of joy and promise.

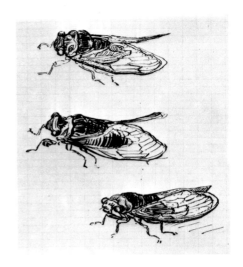

Cicadas   Van Gogh Museum, Amsterdam

Four Flying Swallows   Van Gogh Museum, Amsterdam

Pear Tree in Blossom   Stedelijk Museum, Amsterdam

THE LANGLOIS BRIDGE WITH WOMEN WASHING

The Langlois Bridge at Arles, Staatsgalerie, Stuttgart

As you can see, this bridge could be lowered to allow traffic to pass over or raised so that sailing boats were able to pass through the gap.

Again, as in the previous picture there is a Japanese influence, especially in the direct, simple way van Gogh paints the wooden structure of the bridge itself. In Japanese prints there are many examples of wooden bridges. Almost exactly half way across the bridge a horse and cart, the focal point of the picture, is framed against the blue sky.

The whole scene is saturated with warm sunlight. This warmth is conveyed by van Gogh in glowing orange colours contrasted against the blue coolness of the river reflecting the sky above.

There is contrast too between the hot, quiet stillness of the day and the bustling activity of the women making circular ripples in the water as they wash their clothes.

The Bridge at Langlois, 1888   Los Angeles County Art Museum
Collection of Mr and Mrs George Gard de Sylva

Woman at Table and Woman Standing
Van Gogh Museum, Amsterdam

Langlois Bridge with Women Washing   Kröller-Müller Foundation, Otterlo

LA BERCEUSE

In Arles, van Gogh became friendly with the postman Joseph Roulin, his wife Augustine and their three children. Over a period of time he painted portraits of them all.

The style of this bold and striking portrait of Madame Roulin is in many ways unlike any other he had painted before. Van Gogh greatly admired the work of the painter Paul Gauguin and here we see for the first time his friend's direct influence.

Branches of a Periwinkle
Vincent van Gogh Museum, Amsterdam

The design of the picture, its composition and colour, seem more important than capturing the personality of the sitter. The paintwork is generally much flatter and the modelling of the face and hands less detailed than usual. Without the face and hands the painting would, in fact, begin to look like an abstract pattern. The Japanese print influence is there too in the heavy black line around the figure and chair shape and the decorative wall behind.

Van Gogh was fascinated by his subject and the new technique and painted *La Berceuse* (which means the woman who rocks the cradle) no less than five times. He sent copies to Paul Gauguin and another painter friend, Emile Bernard, as tokens of friendship.

Sunflowers, c1888   National Gallery, London

La Berceuse   Museum of Fine Arts, Boston, Bequest of John T. Spaulding

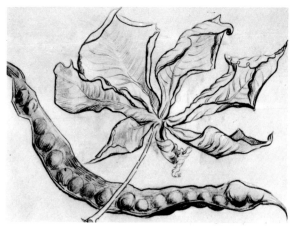

Chestnut Leaf and Husk   Van Gogh Museum, Amsterdam

FRITILLARIES IN A COPPER VASE

The flowers in this painting are so alive they seem to erupt from the copper vase. The effect is rather like a firework flaring in slow motion.

The rich colours of the petals glow luminously among the deep greens and blacks of the stems and leaves. The polished vase below and the surface on which it stands, warmly reflect the reds, oranges and yellows above. In the background bright dots flash like sparks or stars massed in the night sky.

The background is mysterious and without detail to give us any hint of scale. Perhaps this is why the vase and flowers appear to be so large and commanding.

Notice how the two flower heads on the left bend downwards to meet the curved moulding in the vase's centre which, in turn, swings our eye up and around again.

Again, as in so many of van Gogh's paintings, every brush-stroke is visible, revealing the urgency and speed with which he painted.

Fruit Tree and Two People Working   Van Gogh Museum, Amsterdam

Fritillaries in a Copper Vase   The Louvre, Paris

STILL LIFE OF ORANGES AND LEMONS WITH BLUE GLOVES

The oranges and lemons seem to glow internally with the sunlight that ripened them. The small dark green branches of foliage framing the basket contrast with and emphasise the fruits' brightness.

The picture is deceptively simple. Just a basket with a few oranges and lemons in it, a sprig or two and an old pair of gloves. Yet with these ordinary, everyday objects van Gogh expresses the richness of the season and his deep feeling for nature.

Van Gogh represents his own presence in the picture with the pair of gloves. Perhaps something of his personality is conveyed in them in the same way his painting of Gauguin's chair told us much about its owner. Van Gogh always had the ability to invest ordinary objects, furniture, articles of clothing and personal possessions of all kinds, with individual character. They seem to partake of the life of the person to whom they belong.

Figure Sketches Private Collector, New York

Still Life of Oranges and Lemons with Blue Gloves   Collection of Mr and Mrs Paul Mellon

THE STARRY NIGHT

In the valley, the village surrounded by orchards, is peacefully asleep. Soft moonlight illuminates the church, its steeple and the little cluster of houses, and gleams on the tops of the trees. Blue, gentle hills curve protectively around.

Above, in contrast, the night is exploding with energy and movement. Great swirls of light undulate across the sky and huge stars glitter and revolve. A giant, yellow, crescent moon with a shimmering halo climbs over the hills.

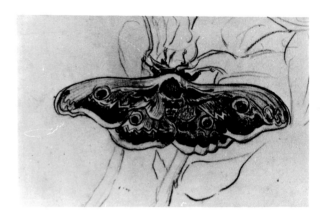

Emperor Moth   Vincent van Gogh Museum, Amsterdam

On the ground, only the cypress tree seems to be awake, rising upwards like a dark flame.

Once again, notice how van Gogh paints with bold separate brushstrokes. In this picture he seems almost to have stabbed the canvas with them so great was his excitement as he worked.

This picture, unlike *Still Life of Oranges and Lemons with Blue Gloves* is painted from memory and with imagination rather than direct observation.

The peaceful landscape seems to represent the ordinary, familiar world and home of man. The brilliant sky expresses the unknowable, awesome power of the universe of which the earth is only a tiny fragment.

Cypresses   The Brooklyn Museum

The Starry Night, 1889   Museum of Modern Art, New York City

PORTRAIT OF DR GACHET

Like van Gogh, Dr Gachet was a very nervous, sometimes sad man. In this portrait his forehead is creased with worry and his eyes seem to look inwards to his unhappy thoughts. One hand supports his weary head, the other rests on the table forgetting the flower close by.

In contrast to the careworn face and figure, the combination of the orange of the table, the green of the flower and the blues in the background, is strong and cheerful.

Dr Gachet was an impatient sitter so van Gogh had to paint quickly. As in *Starry Night* we can clearly see each brushstroke applied with great speed and confidence.

Dr Gachet was himself a painter. In fact he really preferred painting to doctoring. During his lifetime he met and encouraged many artists before they became well known. He was one of the few who immediately recognised and admired van Gogh's work.

Miss Gachet at the Piano   Van Gogh Museum, Amsterdam

Portrait of Doctor Gachet   The Louvre, Paris

Along the Canal   Vincent van Gogh Museum, Amsterdam